DONALDSON WAY ~~SCHOOL~~
430 DONALDSON WAY
AMERICAN CANYON, CA
94503

W9-CTQ-317

DISCARD

$19.95

633.11
LAC

The Biography of Wheat

Jennifer D.B. Lackey

Crabtree Publishing Company
www.crabtreebooks.com

Crabtree Publishing Company
www.crabtreebooks.com

Coordinating editor: Ellen Rodger
Editors: Carrie Gleason, Adrianna Morganelli, L. Michelle Nielsen
Production coordinator: Rosie Gowsell
Production assistance and layout: Samara Parent
Art direction: Rob MacGregor
Photo research: Allison Napier
Prepress technician: Nancy Johnson

Photo Credits: Danita Delimont/Alamy: p. cover; Penny Tweedie/Alamy: p. 9 (top); Robert Harding Picture Library Ltd/Alamy: p. 1; AP Photo/B.K. bangash: p. 17; AP Photo/Nati Harnik: p. 29 (top); AP Photo/David Samson: p. 28 (top); Alinari, Osterreichische Nationalbibliothek, Vienna, Austria/The Bridgeman Art Library: p. 20; Archives Charmet, Bibliotheque des Arts Decoratifs, Paris, France/The Bridgeman Art Library: p. 4; Ashmolean Museum, University of Oxford, UK/The Bridgeman Art Library: p. 16 (bottom); Peabody Essex Museum, Salem, Massachusetts, USA/The Bridgeman Art Library: p. 12; Jonathan Blair/Corbis: p. 8; Corbis: p. 27; Terry W. Eggers/Corbis: p. 7;

Kevin Fleming/Corbis: p. 10; Karl-Heinz Haenel/Corbis: p. 21; Jacqui Hurst/Corbis: p. 15 (bottom); Liu Liqun/Corbis: p. 11 (bottom); W. Wayne Lockwood, M.D./Corbis: p. 31; Lawrence Manning/Corbis: p. 15 (top); The Granger Collection, New York: p. 18, p. 22, p. 23, p. 24, p. 25; istock International: p. 4 (top border), p. 16, p. 19 (bottom right), p. 19 (bottom left), p. 28 (bottom); Reuters/Dipak Kumar JSG/JD: p. 26; Jack Dykinga/Science Source/Photo Researchers Inc.: p. 30. Other images from stock photo Cd.

Cartography: Jim Chernishenko: p. 9

Cover: A farmer unloads harvested wheat from a combine machine into a truck for deliver to a storage facility.

Title page: A smiling farmer carries bundles of harvested wheat on his back in Gulmit, Hunza, northern Pakistan.

Contents: A golden, ripe field of wheat is ready for harvest.

Library and Archives Canada Cataloguing in Publication

Lackey, Jennifer, 1969-
    The biography of wheat / Jennifer Lackey.

(How did that get here?)
Includes index.
ISBN 978-0-7787-2495-7 (bound)
ISBN 978-0-7787-2531-2 (pbk.)

    1. Wheat--Juvenile literature. I. Title. II. Series.

SB191.W5L32 2007   j633.1'1   C2007-900696-5

Library of Congress Cataloging-in-Publication Data

Lackey, Jennifer, 1969-
    The biography of wheat / written by Jennifer Lackey.
        p. cm. -- (How did that get here?)
    Includes index.
    ISBN-13: 978-0-7787-2495-7 (rlb)
    ISBN-10: 0-7787-2495-6 (rlb)
    ISBN-13: 978-0-7787-2531-2 (pb.)
    ISBN-10: 0-7787-2531-6 (pb.)
    1. Wheat--Juvenile literature. 2. Wheat trade--Juvenile literature.
I.
Title. II. Series.

SB191.W5L13 2007
633.1'1--dc22   2007003460

Crabtree Publishing Company

www.crabtreebooks.com   1-800-387-7650

Copyright © **2007 CRABTREE PUBLISHING COMPANY.** All rights reserved. No part of this publication may be reproduced, stored in a retrieval system or be transmitted in any form or by any means, electronic, mechanical, photocopying, recording, or otherwise, without the prior written permission of Crabtree Publishing Company. In Canada: We acknowledge the financial support of the Government of Canada through the Book Publishing Industry Development Program (BPIDP) for our publishing activities.

Published in Canada
Crabtree Publishing
616 Welland Ave.
St. Catharines, ON
L2M 5V6

Published in the United States
Crabtree Publishing
PMB16A
350 Fifth Ave., Suite 3308
New York, NY 10118

Published in the United Kingdom
Crabtree Publishing
White Cross Mills
High Town, Lancaster
LA1 4XS

Published in Australia
Crabtree Publishing
386 Mt. Alexander Rd.
Ascot Vale (Melbourne)
VIC 3032

Contents

Our Daily Bread

Wheat is the edible seed of a kind of grass. Thousands of years ago, wheat grew wild in an area historians call the Fertile Crescent, or the ancient Middle East. Today, wheat is the world's second largest crop, after corn. Like rice, rye, oats, and barley, wheat is a cereal crop. Wheat is used to make many of the foods we eat every day, including breads, cookies, cakes, noodles, and breakfast cereals. The seed of a wheat plant is usually ground into flour before it is made into food. Wheat is nutritious, is easily stored and transported, and can be made into many different products. People all over the world count on wheat as one of their main, or staple, sources of food.

Ancient Wheat

Wheat was one of the first plants **domesticated** by people about 10,000 years ago. It was first grown in the Middle East. Learning to cultivate wheat, or grow it as a crop, instead of just finding and harvesting it in the wild, allowed people to live in large groups and permanent settlements. Before farming, humans hunted and gathered their food. With the right conditions, wheat can be stored for many years. That made it an important food source during the winter when other kinds of food could not be grown. Many ancient civilizations depended on wheat for survival.

▼ *Wheat is a grass that originally grew wild in the Middle East. Today, it is grown in temperate climates all over the world.*

On the Market

Wheat is a commodity. Commodities are things that are traded and sold. Early in its history, wheat was mostly grown and eaten locally. People depended on their wheat because without it, they would starve. Shipping was expensive and many commodities never made it to their destinations. People made sure that they could grow their own wheat and control its use. Today, shipping is more reliable and faster. Wheat growing is concentrated in the places where wheat grows best and wheat is shipped all over the world.

▸ *Bread is made from wheat flour. Bread was one of the first products made from wheat.*

(below) For thousands of years, wheat was planted and harvested by hand. Today, in countries that export wheat, machines plant and harvest enormous fields of wheat.

From Bread to Soap

Almost all baked goods and noodles are made from wheat. People have invented other ways to use wheat. It can be used for cat litter, dog treats, **biodegradable** spoons and forks, soap, and even wheat concrete! The stalks, or stems, of the plant left after the harvest of the seeds are dried and made into straw. Straw is used to feed animals, to make newsprint, and in bricks and building materials. More than 600 million tons of wheat are grown and sold worldwide every year.

What is Wheat?

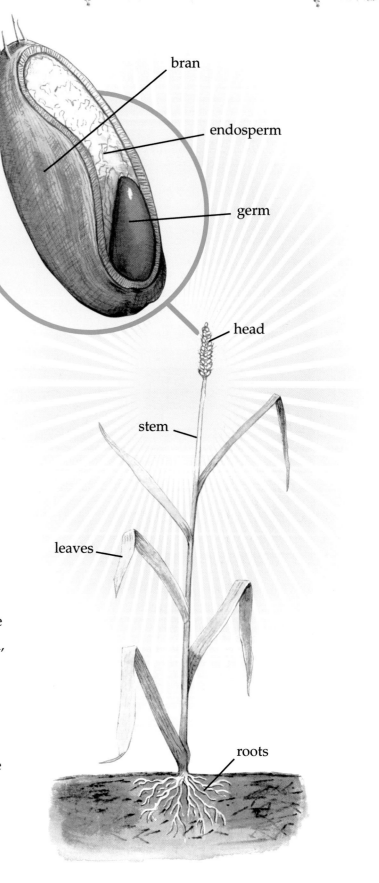

There are thousands of varieties, or types, of wheat. Some varieties developed naturally as wheat grew in different climates around the world, and some varieties were created by humans. Wheat is broken down into several different classes based on the growing season and the characteristics of the seed, or **kernel**. All varieties of wheat have the same basic parts.

The Parts of the Plant

Wheat plants are a kind of grass that grows very tall, usually two feet to four feet (0.6 to 1.2 meters) high. There are four basic parts to the plant: the roots, the stem, the leaves, and the head. The head contains the seeds, or kernels, that people turn into food. The roots take the water and **nutrients** the plant needs from the soil. The stem holds the plant up. The leaves gather energy from the Sun to help the plant grow.

The Parts of the Kernel

The kernel is the seed of the wheat plant. It is the part of the plant that people harvest to make food. It has three parts: the bran, the endosperm, and the germ. The bran covers the kernel. The germ is the part that sprouts into a new plant if the kernel is planted in the ground. The endosperm gives energy to the germ when it is planted, so that it can turn into a new plant. The kernel is sometimes used whole and sometimes broken up into its parts in order to be turned into food.

Varieties of Wheat

The two main kinds of wheat, common wheat (*Triticum aestivum*) and **durum wheat** (*Triticum durum*), have thousands of varieties. The varieties of wheat are classified by when they are planted, the color of their kernels, and the nutrients inside the kernel. Some wheats are planted in winter and some in spring, so they are called either winter wheat or spring wheat. Some wheats are red or white because of the color of their kernels. Some wheats are hard and some are soft. Hard wheats have more **protein** in them, and soft wheats have more **starch**. All durum wheats are hard. A variety of wheat can fall into more than one category at a time. For example, a wheat might be called Hard Red Winter or Soft White Spring. Hard wheats tend to be used for pasta and crusty kinds of bread. Soft wheats tend to be used for pastries, cookies, soft bread, and cakes.

Wheat is the only plant in the world that contains gluten. Gluten is a protein that helps make dough rise.

Where in the World?

Wheat grows in the temperate zones, which are the areas of the world between the tropics and the polar regions. The climate in temperate zones is not prone to extremes of heat or cold. Wheat grows best with 12 to 15 inches (31 to 38 cm) of rain a year and temperatures of 70 to 75° Fahrenheit (21 to 24° C) in the growing season. Wheat also needs a lot of sunshine to grow and it does not grow well in wet, humid climates.

Kinds of Wheat

There are two main types of wheat grown by people all over the world today. The most common one is bread wheat or common wheat. It is used to make bread, cookies, cakes, and some kinds of pasta. The second most common is durum wheat, which is coarser than most kinds of common wheat and is mostly used to make pasta. The two earliest forms of wheat, emmer and einkorn, are rarely grown today.

Farmers harvest wheat grown in the shadow of the Karakoram mountains in northern Pakistan.

Exporters and Importers

Nearly 36 percent of the world's wheat is grown in Asia. Europe grows 17 percent of the world's wheat and North America grows 16 percent. Selling and buying wheat is big business. The biggest grower and the biggest importer of wheat is China. China has so many people that it cannot grow all the wheat it needs. China buys wheat from other countries, mainly from North America. North America also exports wheat to the **European Union** and Japan. Government rules and customer preferences in these countries can affect what kinds of wheat are grown in North America. For example, people in Europe and Japan do not want to buy **genetically modified** wheat because they feel that it is not safe. This has prevented farmers in the United States and Canada from growing these kinds of wheat for export.

▼ *A farmer sifts kernels of winter wheat grown in Yunnan, China.*

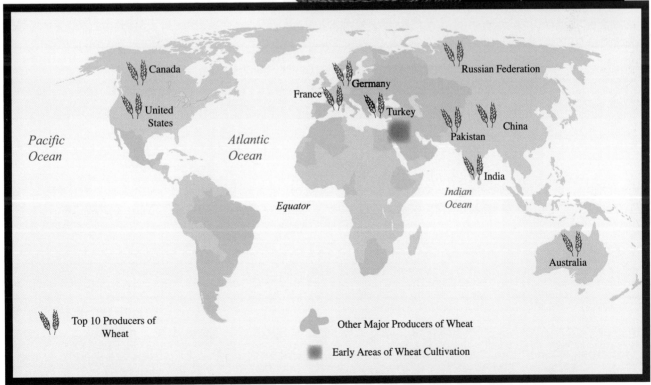

(above) *Wheat first grew wild, and was later cultivated, or grown as a crop, in the Middle East. Today, it grows throughout the world.*

Growing Wheat

A farmer prepares his wheat field for planting. Some wheat is sown, or planted, in the spring and others in the fall.

Wheat is grown from the same seeds, or kernels, that people eat. Ancient farmers saved part of their seed to be planted the following year. In parts of the world where **subsistence farming** takes place, farmers still keep some seed aside in case of poor or destroyed crops and droughts. On large commercial farms, where wheat is grown for sale or export, farmers still sometimes save seed from previous years or they buy seed each year from seed companies. Bought seed introduces new varieties of wheat and it is sometimes considered "cleaner" than saved seed, which means that it has no extra seeds from weeds included in it. It is more expensive to buy new seed every year.

Sowing Time

Before farmers can plant, or sow, the seed, they must prepare their fields. They add nutrients to the soil, or plant different kinds of crops before they plant their wheat to make sure the soil is healthy and fertile. When they are ready to plant, some farmers till the soil with a plow. Tilling is breaking the soil up so it is soft enough for the seeds to take root. Any weeds growing in the field are killed by tilling. Once the field has been tilled, the farmers plant their seeds, often with a grain drill. The grain drill is a machine that opens a little ditch in the soil, drops the seed in to the right depth, and covers the seed up with more soil. Before machinery was invented, all these steps were done by hand with small tools.

Amber Waves of Grain

Once the seeds are planted, they start to develop root systems. The roots take water and nutrients out of the soil so that the plant can use them and the seed begins to grow a stem and some leaves. Soon, the stem and the leaves are big enough to pop out of the soil. The leaves unfurl and the young plant is visible above the ground. The green color of the leaves is caused by **chlorophyll**. Chlorophyll allows plants to use the Sun's energy to help them grow.

▲ *Wheat kernels, or seeds, can be eaten or planted to grow a crop.*

(below) Wheat is grown in many areas of the world, including this mountain valley in Tibet.

Threats to the Crop

While the plants are growing, many things can happen that might ruin the crop. If not enough rain falls, the plants will not have enough water to survive. Strong storms can knock the plants over and ruin the heads. Insects, such as aphids and armyworms, might attack the wheat and eat it. Different kinds of fungi are the main threat to growing wheat. A fungus is a kind of disease that attacks the stem and the leaves of the plant. It destroys the stems and the chlorophyll in the leaves. Fungus prevents the heads of the plant from growing properly. If the infection is bad enough, the whole crop may be lost. Farmers have many different ways to try to kill insects and fungi if their crops are attacked. These methods do not always work.

Poisoned Flour Fungus

Ergot is one kind of fungus that can grow on wet kernels, even after a crop has been harvested. When the infected kernels are made into flour and then into bread, the ergot gets into the bread and people eat it. The people who eat the bread can become very sick. Ergot poisoning can cause people to hallucinate, or see or imagine things that did not happen. It can also cause convulsions, seizures, and vomiting. This is what happened in Salem, Massachusetts, in 1692, when several young girls mysteriously became ill. They had convulsions and seemed to be talking to people or things that were not there. People did not have the medical knowledge that they have today, so no one was sure what had happened to them. People believed that witches must have cast spells on the girls and several townspeople were accused of witchcraft. Twenty-five people were put on trial, found guilty, and executed for supposedly being witches. This event, called the Salem Witch Trials, is a very famous part of the history of the United States. With current knowledge of plant diseases, people today believe that the girls' sickness was caused by ergot poisoning of grains grown in the Salem area.

▾ *Scientists today know that grain poisoned by ergot causes people to hallucinate. The Salem area had several rainy growing seasons prior to 1692, the year the witch trials took place. Salem was a very religious place, so when the hallucinations could not be explained, people were accused of practicing witchcraft.*

Harvest Time

As wheat grows, it begins to develop kernels at the head of the plant. The kernels ripen until they are ready to be harvested. Depending on the climate and the type of wheat being grown, it can take about five months from when the wheat is planted until it is ready to be harvested. Winter wheat take longer, and spring wheat are ready sooner, especially when they are planted in warm places. When the heads begin to droop over and the kernels are dry, it is harvest time.

Combines are expensive machines that save farmers a lot of time because they "combine" three harvesting processes.

Separating Wheat From Chaff

Until the mid-1800s, people used to walk through the fields using curved blades called sickles to cut the heads off the wheat. They then tied the wheat together in bundles. Next, the wheat was threshed, or beaten until the kernels came loose from the stem and the rest of the head. The papery covering of the kernels, called chaff, was removed by tossing the kernels into the air on a windy day. The wind blew the lightweight chaff away and the heavier kernels fell to the ground into a basket. This process is called winnowing. Winnowing was time-consuming work. In some countries, wheat is still winnowed this way.

Combine Machines

Today, commercial farmers use a combine machine to thresh and winnow. A combine cuts the wheat from the stems in the fields, threshes and winnows the kernels, and then pours the kernels into a big bin to be hauled away to be stored or sold.

From Seed to Supper

Once the wheat is harvested, it still has a long way to go before it ends up on our tables. Harvested wheat is usually stored in a silo or a grain elevator. It is called a grain elevator because it has a platform that moves the wheat up off the floor. This helps keep the wheat from getting wet and spoiling. Different varieties of wheat are kept separate from one another so that the companies buying the wheat will be able to choose exactly what they want. Different kinds of wheat are used to make different kinds of flour. When the wheat is finally sold, it goes from the silo or grain elevator to a factory where it is turned into the right kind of flour.

From Kernels to Flour

Once it gets to the flour factory, the wheat is inspected to make sure that it is the right quality. The kernels are run through screens and sifted many times to remove stones, sticks, or anything else that is not a wheat kernel.

(right) The North American prairies, or plains, are wheat-growing areas dotted with grain silos and elevators. Often, the elevators are located near railroad tracks as the grain was once commonly transported to shipping ports by rail car.

Whole Wheat Flour

Once the kernels are clean, what happens next depends on what kind of flour is being made. Whole wheat flour is made from whole kernels of wheat that are ground up into flour, which is then sacked, and sold to stores and bakeries. All the parts of the kernel - the bran, the germ, and the endosperm - are smashed together and used. The germ and the bran have nutrients in them. The endosperm by itself does not. This makes whole wheat flour healthy, but it is also coarse.

White Flour

If white flour is being made, the cleaned kernels are run through a series of rollers. The rollers squeeze and break the wheat kernels so that the bran, the endosperm, and the germ are broken apart and separated. The broken kernels are then sifted. The bran, the germ, and the endosperm end up in three separate bins. The germ and the bran are sold separately to make breakfast cereal and other things. The endosperm is ground up into white flour.

(top) A woman threshes grain by hand.

(above) Some flour is bleached to make it look whiter.

15

Flour Mills

Before the invention of complicated sifting and grinding machines, people had to grind flour by hand. At first, the grain was ground together with stones. Eventually, people invented water-powered mills, where the rushing water of a river turned millstones that ground the kernels into flour. People grew their own wheat and then took it to a mill, where the miller ground their grain into flour and then gave it back. If white flour was being made, the miller sifted the parts of the kernel before doing the final fine grinding. The miller was usually given a portion of the grain as payment.

Other Kinds of Flour

Wheat is not the only kind of plant that is made into flour. Many other kinds of grains, nuts, and seeds can be ground into flour as well. Rice, beans, and potatoes are often made into flour. These kinds of flour do not have gluten, the substance in wheat kernels that makes bread fluffy and light. Bread made with non-wheat flours is often very heavy and dense.

(top right) Many old mills still exist, but most no longer grind flour. These mills are called gristmills. Grist means ground grain.

The Wheat Market

The amount of wheat grown every year depends on weather, insects, and diseases. Growing wheat can be a risky business. When wheat farmers have a bad crop, they have less wheat to sell and they make less money. When wheat farmers have a good crop, a lot of wheat is available on the market. They have more wheat to sell, but that drives down the price. Instead of getting more money for growing more wheat, they get less.

◄ A quern was a type of stone used for grinding grain. This ancient tool is called a saddle quern.

Wheat Subsidies

Many countries believe that growing wheat is good for their **economy**. To encourage farmers to grow wheat in spite of the risks, the countries pay their farmers to grow wheat. This payment is called a subsidy. In countries with subsidies, the farmers get the price of the wheat they sell and then an additional payment of cash on top of the selling price. The European Union, the United States, Canada, and many other countries have wheat subsidies.

▾ *Wheat is often used in international aid programs, where aid is given by wealthier countries to poorer countries. Sometimes, a poorer country is given money but it must buy agricultural products, such as wheat, from the country giving the money. This system is called "tied aid."*

Wheat Boards

To help wheat farmers get the best prices for their crops, some countries, including Canada and Australia, have established wheat boards or councils. A wheat board is a government organization that controls the price of wheat. All the farmers in that country sell the wheat to the wheat board, which then sets the price of wheat. Instead of all the farmers competing against each other to try to sell their wheat, everyone sells all their wheat and gets the same price no matter what. This system is meant to ensure that farmers can sell their wheat and get a good price for it every year no matter how much wheat is available.

The History of Wheat

Many thousands of years ago, people did not grow food of their own. They wandered from place to place, hunting animals and gathering food from the plants they found around them. When they used up all the food in one area, they moved on. Around 10,000 to 12,000 years ago, people living in the Fertile Crescent, an area known today as the Middle East, learned how to plant and harvest a grass that grew wild.

A Farming Revolution

Over time, the wild grass developed into wheat. Wheat was among the first crops that people grew. Planting, growing, and harvesting a crop allowed humans to live permanently in one area. Permanent settlement for farming changed the way humans lived. Scientists believe the first farmers grew einkorn wheat and emmer wheat and boiled the kernels to make a porridge.

Wheat Spreads

By about 5,000 years ago, both kinds of wheat had spread to southern Europe, northern Africa, and India. The ancient Egyptians may have been the first people to make leavened, or raised, bread similar to what we eat today. The workers who built the pyramids in Egypt were paid in bread. Historians believe that wheat was brought to China through trade and immigration around 1500 B.C. The Chinese used wheat mostly for making noodles.

▶ *The Roman Goddess Ceres with a wheat sheaf.*

Making and Breaking Bread

The ancient Greeks and Romans depended upon wheat for food. They developed a taste for white bread. The Greeks were the first to make pastries and cakes sweetened with honey. The Romans had several different kinds of bread and bakers who baked only bread. Roman politicians sometimes gave bread away to the poor. By the time of the end of the Roman Empire, around 1,500 years ago, wheat had spread to large parts of Europe, Asia, and North Africa.

Leavened or Unleavened?

Leavening is the process that makes the bread we eat today fluffy and light. Baking soda and baking powder are two common leavening agents, but the best and most common leavening agent is yeast. Yeast is a kind of fungus that converts the energy in bread dough into gas. This gas makes tiny balloons of air all through the bread dough. The dough then rises, or gets bigger. It becomes lighter because it is filled with small pockets of air. Without yeast or some other kind of leavening agent, bread does not rise. Unleavened bread is flat and dense, like a pancake or a cracker. Before people learned to make leavened bread, all the bread that people ate was unleavened. Many people continued to eat unleavened bread even after leavening was invented because it takes more work and time to make leavened bread. The ancient Egyptians were the first to make leavened bread. People did not know about yeast then, but the ancient Egyptians discovered that if they left their bread dough out in the open air, it would eventually rise by itself. This happened because natural yeasts in the air would fall into the dough and begin to grow.

▲ *Most of the commercial bread sold in markets and grocery stores is leavened, or yeast raised. Some leavened bread, such as sourdough bread, is made from dough that is fermented and saved from a previous batch.*

◀ *Pita, crackers, nan bread, and flour tortillas are just a few examples of unleavened, or yeast-less bread.*

Wheat in Europe

By the Middle Ages, a period of time from 500 to 1500 A.D., food made from wheat was the most important food in Europe, particularly for the poor. People still ate flat, unleavened cakes and porridges, but leavened bread was the most common. Many people worked on farms and needed quick, nourishing meals. It was easy to take a hunk of bread into the fields to eat at lunch. At meals, people often put meats, sauces, and soups on top of bread plates called trenchers. When people were done eating the main dish, they ate the bread plate.

Most people did not have ovens in their homes, so the village baker did the baking for everyone. The ovens were heated by wood and often located away from the village so that if a fire broke out, it would not spread everywhere.

Bread and Politics

Bread was so important to the poor of Europe that countries often made laws about how much bread could cost. If bread became too expensive, the working people would starve. Without workers, other crops and goods could not be produced. Not all the bread that the poor ate was made with wheat. Wheat was more expensive than other grains, such as barley. The lighter the flour, the more work it took to produce it and the more expensive it was. White bread became the bread of the rich. In times of war and famine, wheat and bread became very precious. If bread ran out, riots and revolutions could be the result. It is no wonder that when Europeans began coming to the New World, or North, South, and Central America, they brought their wheat with them.

Crop Rotation

By the Middle Ages, farmers learned that allowing part of their fields to lie fallow, or rest, every year increased their yields of grain. Every year they switched the planted field and the fallow field. This was called two-field crop rotation. By the 1500s, farmers were using three-field crop rotation. Wheat was planted in one field, beans or barley were planted in the second, and the third part was left fallow. The beans or barley helped replace nutrients in the soil, so yields stayed high. By the 1600s, farmers were using four-field crop rotation, which used all of the field all the time. The four parts of the field grew wheat, barley, clover, and turnips. Every year, a different crop was grown in each field so the nutrients in the soil were replenished.

A yellow rape field grows next to a field of unripe wheat. Rape is a type of seed in the mustard family.

21

New World Wheat

Wheat first came to the New World with the Spanish in the late 1400s and early 1500s. It was not until the first permanent European colonies were successful in the 1600s, that wheat began to be grown on a large scale. Before the arrival of Europeans, **indigenous** people in North America relied mostly on corn, or maize, and beans as their main food.

Old World Crop in a New World

The long harsh winters in eastern North America made growing wheat more difficult than it was in the more temperate parts of Europe. European colonists did not want to give up eating bread, so they grew as much wheat as they could. Wheat was likely grown at **Port Royal** in the early 1600s. During the British colonial period of Canadian history, Ontario became a wheat producer.

Northern Colonial Wheat

The climate in the New England colonies of Rhode Island, Connecticut, Massachusetts, and New Hampshire was too cold and wet for wheat to grow well. People grew as much wheat as they could, but they relied on other crops such as corn, rye, and beans. They made bread from corn flour and rye flour, as well as from wheat flour. Most of all, they relied on fish and other kinds of meats. The middle colonies of the United States - Delaware, Pennsylvania, New Jersey, and New York - were the best farming lands. Wheat grew fairly well there. When wheat prices were high in Europe because of population increases or wars, like in the mid 1700s, colonists even grew enough wheat to sell in Europe for a profit.

Harvesting wheat in the colonies was hard work. Farmers used sickles to cut grain by hand.

Southern Plantations

The southern colonies of the United States - Maryland, Virginia, Georgia, North Carolina, and South Carolina - concentrated on growing crops to sell for money. In the early to mid-1700s, they grew a lot of tobacco. U.S. president George Washington's farm in Virginia started out growing tobacco, but he realized that growing wheat made more sense. If the market for selling tobacco was bad one year and prices were low, farmers had no choice but to try to sell the tobacco for whatever money they could get. A whole field full of tobacco was no use to the farmer. Wheat was always useful, even in years when wheat prices were low. A farmer could hold on to wheat for another year and see if prices improved, because wheat stored well.

Wheat Exports

By the mid-to-late 1800s, many of the new plains states such as Kansas and Missouri were growing wheat. The Canadian prairie provinces of Manitoba, Saskatchewan, and Alberta, became "bread baskets," or major wheat-growing areas in the early-to-mid-1900s. New wheat strains, adapted to European **steppes** and grasslands, grew very well in these places. The North American grassland climate was warm in the spring and summer and usually received the right amount of rain to grow wheat. The United States and Canada began to be major exporters of wheat to the rest of the world.

(above) A farm girl brings a jug of water to a harvest crew in the 1800s.

The Dust Bowl

World War I meant farming in Europe was disrupted by fighting. At the same time, worldwide demand for wheat increased. Many men who would normally have tended crops were fighting in the war. North America began growing more wheat to fill the need. Before this time, most prairie land was covered with wild prairie grass that needed little water. As the demand for wheat grew, the prairie grass was tilled over. Wheat, which needed more water than prairie grass, was planted. Crops were not rotated because demand for wheat was so great. As the war ended and the 1920s began, farmers began using gasoline-powered tractors instead of animals in their fields. This allowed fewer people to work more land.

A Decade of Drought

In 1929, a drought struck the plains of the United States and Canada. It would be five years before very much rain fell, and ten years before the drought was completely over. As the soil became drier and drier, the wheat and other crops died. Dust storms blew soil through windows and doors. Instead of North America's Breadbasket, the plains and prairies became the **Dust Bowl**.

(below) Years of drought turned wheat farms into dust-farms. The drought coincided with the Great Depression, a time of little economic growth and great poverty in the 1930s. Dust storms blackened the skies over prairie towns.

The Great Depression

During the same time as the drought, the economies of most of the world's countries began losing money. Factories closed and many people lost their jobs. This period of time was known as the Great Depression. The Depression lasted until the beginning of World War II in 1939. Between the drought and the Depression, life in the North American prairies was very grim.

(above) The southern plains of the United States were hardest hit by the drought, and Oklahoma was one of the most desperate areas. So many of the people moving to California were from Oklahoma that people moving west came to be called "Okies." Some historians estimate that 15 percent of the population of Oklahoma had moved west by 1939.

Moving Out

Many prairie farmers whose fields had blown away could not find any other work. The Canadian and United States governments both developed plans to help the poor, but many people felt lost and hungry. Some farmers decided that the only way to improve their lives was to move out of the prairies for good. By the mid-1930s, things were so bad in the plains that many people just packed up the things they could carry and moved. Families left their dried-up farms to look for work elsewhere. Many became migrant workers, picking up whatever work they could in order to feed their families. Others chose to go west because they thought of it as a land of gold and warmer weather. This westward migration was one of the largest changes in population within the United States in history.

The Green Revolution

Between 1940 and about 1975, new ways of growing crops allowed people to grow more food on the same amount of land. This period of time is called the **Green Revolution**. Several different **technologies** were developed that changed the way that people grew wheat.

Hybrid Wheat

A hybrid plant is a blend of two different types of plants. In the early 1900s, scientists began to find ways of using the natural life cycle of wheat to produce wheat hybrids. By blending two different types of wheat together, they could create a new kind of wheat. They gradually increased the amount of seed that each wheat plant produced. They also created plants that were more **resistant** to insects and diseases.

Man-made Fertilizer

People have fertilized, or put extra nutrients in the soil, since the very beginning of agriculture. For thousands of years, the nutrients came from natural sources in the environment, such as plants and animal dung. The substances used to add nutrients are called fertilizers because they make the soil more fertile. During the Green Revolution, scientists learned how to create fertilizers artificially. These artificial fertilizers forced more nutrients into the soil than the old natural methods and made the plants grow faster and larger.

(above) Farmers sprinkle chemical fertilizer on their wheat crop in Ropar in the northern Indian state of Punjab.

Man-Made Pesticides

One of the big problems facing farmers was how to get rid of pests that attacked their plants. Pests such as insects, fungi, bacteria, viruses, or even other plants can keep crops from growing well. Sometimes whole fields of crops can die from pests. Before the Green Revolution, farmers had some ways of handling pests, like moving their crops so that insects did not come back to the same field year after year for the same food. Their methods did not always work very well. Green Revolution scientists invented different chemical sprays called pesticides to kill the insects, weeds, and other pests without harming the crops. Pesticides were easier to use and stronger than the old methods of pest control.

▾ *Before modern combines were invented, harvesting was a time-consuming process involving many men and teams of horses.*

Irrigation

Irrigation is moving water from a river, stream, or well to fields to water crops. It is necessary in places where there is not enough rain and during droughts. Farmers have been irrigating their fields since at least 6000 B.C. During the Green Revolution, people started using motors to pump large amounts of water for irrigation systems, sometimes over long distances. This allowed more land to be irrigated and more crops to be grown. Wheat does not require as much water as some other crops, but in very dry places, irrigation can increase the amount of wheat that farmers can grow. With irrigation, farmers began to harvest four times as much wheat from the same amount of land.

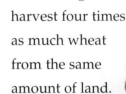

COMBINED HARVESTER   NO 1063
PHOTO
BY W A RAYMOND   MORO ORE

Wheat Threats and Hopes

Wheat plants and wheat farmers face many challenges, from bad weather to changes in the way wheat is farmed. A good crop depends on good weather. If enough rain does not fall, the plants will not have enough water to survive. Too much rain will drown the roots and make plants susceptible to disease. Strong wind and hail can knock the plants over and ruin the heads.

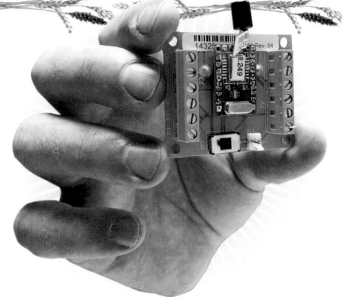

▲ *A wireless sensor warns of drought and disease in the fields.*

Insect Invasion

Aphids are the biggest insect problem for wheat farmers. Aphids are tiny insects that suck the sap out of the stem of wheat plants. Without sap, the plants cannot get nutrients and water from the soil and they die. Hessian flies lay their eggs on the leaves of wheat. When the eggs hatch, the larvae, or immature flies, suck the sap out of the wheat stems. Sometimes farmers spray **insecticide** to kill these insects.

Wheat Diseases

The diseases that wheat farmers worry about most are fungi. A fungus usually destroys the stems and leaves. Leaf rust, black stem rust, and loose smut are some common types of fungal diseases in wheat. Wheat can also be infected by viruses, which are often carried by insects.

(left) Ladybugs eat other harmful insects.

Organic Wheat

Organic food is food that is grown without using artificial pesticides and fertilizers. Some people believe that these methods leave residues in food that are not good for people. Organic farmers grow wheat using methods that people used before the Green Revolution. They put nutrients back into the soil by using crop rotation and adding things that occur naturally in the environment to the soil. Organic farmers will sometimes release "helpful" insects such as ladybugs and lacewings into their field to eat the harmful insects. They pull weeds up by hand or use other natural methods to get rid of weeds. While most people believe that organic farming produces less food than Green Revolution methods, some recent studies have suggested that well-managed organic farms can produce the same amount of food as large-scale commercial farms.

▲ Pizza made from refined white flour that has the same nutrients as whole wheat flour.

Bioengineering vs. Hybridization

Hybridization is how new strains of wheat were created until the late 1990s. Bioengineering is a new process. Bioengineering is an artificial process that makes changes directly to a plant's **DNA**. Hybridization creates new kinds of plants by using the plant's natural life cycle. Hybridization can change some properties of a plant, such as how much seed it produces, or how much water it needs, but it is slower and the amount of change that can be made is smaller. Bioengineering can make very large changes in plants very quickly.

◀ Bioengineering is a new science. Some people worry about unknown negative effects, such as food allergies or diseases, of bioengineered foods on people who eat them.

29

The Future of Wheat

Wheat has been an important part of people's lives for thousands of years. As our world changes in the future, wheat will probably change along with it.

Organic Growing

More and more people are buying organic food or foods grown without chemicals. Organic farming requires farmers to use natural pesticides and fertilizers. Many countries have rules that organic farmers must follow. Farmers growing wheat organically must rotate their crops to ensure that the soil is fertile. Organic wheat must also be stored in a silo that has not stored wheat grown with the use of chemicals. Organic wheat is not yet grown in the quantities of wheat grown with chemicals.

Bioengineered Wheat

Bioengineered wheat is wheat that has been genetically modified to be resistant to pests and diseases. The plant's genetic structure has been altered with chemicals and the genes of other plants. Environmental groups have opposed genetically engineered wheat because they believe not enough is known about the wheat and the long term effects of eating products made with it. Many farmers are reluctant to grow genetically modified wheat because the buyers for their wheat in Europe and Japan do not want it. Seed and chemical companies that make bioengineered wheat seeds say it is perfectly safe.

◄ *Wheat seeds treated with bacteria make them immune from a fungus.*

Fossil Fuel Shortages

One challenge to today's methods of large-scale farming might come from a lack of **fossil fuels**. There are only so many tons of fossil fuels that exist in the world. When those reserves are used up, people will not be able to get any more. Some scientists believe that we may run out of fossil fuels within the next one hundred years. If that is true, then there will not be enough fossil fuel to make the artificial pesticides and fertilizers for farms, nor enough gasoline to drive the big tractor machines that commercial farms need. When the country of Cuba could no longer get fossil fuels and artificial pesticides and fertilizers from the Soviet Union, it changed its farming methods. Now Cuban farms use mostly older farming methods and have gone back to using more animals to pull machinery. Perhaps in the future, shortages of fossil fuels will force other countries to follow Cuba's lead.

Global Warming

Most scientists believe that our planet is getting warmer and warmer every year. This process is called global warming. If this warming continues, the climate will change. Some places that are dry now may become wetter, and places that are wet may become drier. If that happens, then the places that grow wheat now may not be able to continue to grow it in the future. Countries that depend on wheat for a large part of their economy would have to find something to replace wheat farming or their economies would start to collapse. Countries that do not grow wheat today might be able to start growing a lot of wheat.

(above) Three combines harvest a wheat field. Farm machinery are run on fossil fuels, which contributes to global warming.

Glossary

biodegradable Something that degrades, or breaks down over time

chlorophyll The green color in leaves and plants that converts the Sun's energy into growth

DNA The shortened name for deoxyribonucleic acid, the material found in the cells of everything alive

domesticated A plant or animal that is no longer wild and is adapted to human care

durum wheat A wheat often used to make flour for pasta

Dust Bowl A region, such as the central United States during the 1930s, that is extremely dry because of drought and dust storms

economy The economic system and industry of a country or region

European Union An organization of European countries formed to make trade easier

fossil fuel A fuel, such as oil, coal, and natural gas, made from ancient decomposed plant and animal matter

genetically modified Plants or animals that have been bred or created with changes made to their genetic structures

Great Depression A worldwide economic downturn that started in October 1929 and lasted until the beginning of World War I

Green Revolution The increase in the world production of cereals such as wheat and rice during the 1960s and 1970s because of better seed and new agricultural technology

indigenous Originating in a particular region

insecticide A substance used for killing insects

kernel The softer, usually edible, part contained in the shell of a nut or seed

nutrient A source of nourishment, or something that is good for you

Port Royal The first settlement in Canada; now known as Annapolis Royal

protein A nutrient found in plants and animals, needed for muscle growth

resistant Able to resist or stand up to something

starch A nutrient found mostly in plants that provides energy

steppes Dry, grass-covered lands

subsistence farming Farming that provides enough food for the farmer but not for sale

technologies The use of scientific knowledge to create a solution

World War I An international conflict that took place in Europe and lasted from 1914 to 1918

Index

Printed in the U.S.A.